THROUGH THE STONECUTTER'S WINDOW

ALSO BY INDIGO MOOR

Tap-Root (book of poetry)

The Displaced Child (chapbook)

INDIGO MOOR

Through the Stonecutter's Window

Poems

Northwestern University Press
Evanston, Illinois

Northwestern University Press
www.nupress.northwestern.edu

Printed in the United States of America

10 9 8 7 6 5 4 3 2 1

Library of Congress Cataloging-in-Publication Data

Moor, Indigo.
    Through the stonecutter's window : poems / Indigo Moor.
        p. cm.
    Poems, some previously published.
    ISBN 978-0-8101-2699-2 (pbk. : alk. paper)
    I. Title.
    PS3613.O5535T48 2010
    811'.6—dc22

                                           2009049636

♾ The paper used in this publication meets the minimum requirements of the
American National Standard for Information Sciences—Permanence of Paper
for Printed Library Materials, ANSI Z39.48-1992.

Title page image: Shutterstock copyright © Tuchka.

For Heather, Damian, and Savannah

Of course, I know the stone cutters, at least in Baltimore old slang: *stone* as adjective for very sure, definite, an observation to be trusted; *cutter* as in expert dancer, which involves lines and feet and rhythm, beating out competition.

—CHARLES LYNCH

CONTENTS

MIDAFTERNOON

DUSK

ACKNOWLEDGMENTS

The following poems have appeared in *Arkansas Review, The Blue Moon Literary & Arts Review, Cave Canem Anthology X, Poems-For-All,* or *Suisun Valley Review:*

> After
>
> The Argument
>
> Glass
>
> Grasshopper Blues
>
> Growing Wings
>
> Halo in Decline
>
> Holding Patterns
>
> The Homecoming: Brother
>
> The Homecoming: Father
>
> The Homecoming: Prodigal
>
> Hummingbird's Clothing
>
> Malaise
>
> Marking Time Blues
>
> Messages from the Ether
>
> Mississippi Barbecue
>
> Moonlighting
>
> Never Come Home Again

One Summer

Perspective, Wanting

Plain Sight

The Procurer

Puertas Abiertas

Rebirth

Thief

The (Un)doing

Veiled Vision

Special thanks to:

Toni Wynn

Star Vaughn

Sacramento Poetry Center

Stonecoast MFA Program

THROUGH THE STONECUTTER'S WINDOW

DAYBREAK

Night seeds shadows, crevices them
into my subconscious. Now, breaks
swiftly, the dawn. Dreams ride
bareback the day's light: clarity
or madness? Illumination or insanity?

The Procurer

Lucian Freud's The Procurer:
Man in a Headscarf

By God, it could
      be anything:
a vase, curved
or a candlestick, slender

this person you lessen,
intensely, with such
      mute articulation
piece by piece
   by inch and avarice.

But always
   your title demands:
   this acquisition
      must be female.

Your fleshy nose probes
the crooked ways.

Lucian gave you
his uncle's eyes—tender
   wicked seeds
      that pockmark
your face—dark

orbs set aslant above
the raw, puffed cheeks;
skin alternately stroked,
                violent pinks
and translucent grays.

Fixated upon you
    —as you, I—
perhaps canvas
    is the portal by
which you view me

as valued product
        of oils and thinners.

Cloaked as clergy
swaddled
    in ocher headscarf
your lips pursed
to suit

as if in prayer;

though
if you are priest
your all-encompassing
head
    the heaven-seal
        that binds the world
then

I am cast off rosary
        beyond sin
        beyond sin and hope
        beyond sin and hope
and prayer

Always, I am left
        whispering,
my tongue fingering
your name:

            The Procurer

        gatherer
        provider of flesh.

For hours, for days
for those truculent lips
I keep a despairing vigil:

waiting
        for the moment
when that dark-hinged gate

            swings open—exit
            the solemn breath—

the choice, the damned:

"That one. *Her.*"

Moonlighting

The circus now packed
      in mothballs and crates
for the winter,
                  tigers stowed,
elephants anchored
                  to dust.

Down from my perch
removed from bright
      lights, I am
nothing. Certainly,
                  no longer

the *Tattooed, Albino*
Snake-Man, not
      with popcorn machines
rusting, cork-loaded
popguns hibernating,
                  unpolished.

Today, I am just a thin-tall
freak sipping Earl
Grey, natty
            housecoat &
slippers, house shades drawn.

Mesmerized
        by TV (no
sound) news of

    The Little Girl
Trapped 30 feet
        beneath earth,

devoured by hunger:
        the open maw
of a ghost-dry well.

No fireman
no policeman
no holyman
        can reach her.

Savor the tension
        hands wringing.
All that's missing
    is big-top glare.

On-screen, exasperated,
        the sheriff
    picks up a phone
to call, finally

me

an albino thin-tall
        carny, sipping
tea, not surprised

by the phone
jarring, vibrating
          away the silence.

Maybe
     superstition makes me
          the last person
called or
               perhaps

it's the scarlet robe
          I theatrically cast
off my illustrated skin

carnival freak-show
attraction
          turned savior:

Snake!
               Man!
Molting!

     once more,
          body a supple
tongue twisting
     along forbidden paths.

Ankles bound
the crane hoists
     my graffitied
body: slender white snake
               twisting down

toward the well's
    steady, gaping mouth.

    The crowd's single
head sways up
    to me, naturally,
        I am the sun.

In stuttering
      camera flash
dragons & snakes
    coil
      then leap!
from my skin.

                —for Patricia Smith

Puertas Abiertas

Oil on canvas by Marcos Rosales

Understanding
    the hubris inherent
in Dorian Gray's
psyche, you paint
    flesh with flesh,
cast heart pulp down
as if it were *Toro Bravo.*

Slowly pump
varying shades,
    red across the four
chambers of canvas.
                 Always

mindful of the shaman's
warning: *Never*
        sell this original.

In all its frangibility
enfolding, brittle
       synthesis
    of blood and fervor
we are reminded:

this is your chest split-
          ripe, the heart
     still beating
like a blacksmith's forge.

Royal chestnut
     bleeds into dark
Venetian
     top to bottom
as your strokes

contract and relax
diastole
     & systole, piston
work of your passion.

Through your left
     and right atriums,
          thick crimson ripples,
raised in relief,
     hold court with
an orange Cordoban hat,
          throbbing like
an autumn sun.

Below, calming fervor
is woven into ventricles:
          flamenco boots
in blurred motion.

A noose-thin tie
laid flat, restrains
     a wan
          river cascading.

15

And all the while
the canvas tinged
        with undulating waves

as if
        (in afterthought) you
offer up your trackwork
        of nerves in sacrifice,
pulsing
        with cryptic lightning.

Hummingbird's Clothing

I am all wing and hollowed bone
strung together with frayed nerves.
No, I am not darting aimlessly—
my job, thankless, is to connect
your backyard's invisible braille,
while tilting, drunk on scarlet nectar.

Lean close to hear my buzzing
revelation: I am an Anger God!

Praying for a brawl, a brother
to fly too close and reveal me:
King of the low-hung sky! Each
wingbeat jackhammers the day
into submission as the sweet breath
detonates on my savage tongue!

Veiled Vision

Acrylic by Katie Caulk

Anchored—as his tired
                bones insisted—
        to the chair, sunken
into a cashmere coat
with thick raised collar,

you had no choice
        but to swirl his weight
onto the wicker armrest.

You give us Monet,
        subtracted by everything
he no longer is:

        cataracts stacking
behind shades; shrunken
skull plastered

beneath the brim
            of a gaudy sunhat.

No wonder
he succumbed to this pose:

Camille, Alice, and Jean
      are dead fading as his days
and his eyesight.

Gently he rocks—
      the cottage before
him, the bridge after—
off the focus
            of the canvas.

I can almost see you
            pyrrhically calling
brilliant stroke and heroic light
      to take arms
against the dying
            of Claude's seasons.

Yet, not even your signature
resembling a Roman
      numeral IX can resurrect
feline litheness
            into his body.

Of the futility he must sense
            in you, the bemused
tilt of his head says
      all we need to know.

Beneath the light-
            soaked beard are lips
pressed to keep
                  the secret
      you are desperate
to protect us from:

19

a day will come
        for each of us
when we are nothing
            more than still life
        in another's eyes.

—*for Carl Phillips*

Plain Sight

From an interview with an artist's model

You sloughed off
           a bad marriage
           youth
           every stitch
                of clothing—

until you are naked beneath
           the cleansing bright heat
of track lighting.

Legs and arms
        strike cubist angles
while students work
from light to dark.

Brushes swiftly arc through
your five-minute poses.

The buzzer sounds.

Your hands unplant
from thinning hips,
    stretch and grasp air,
hang from
           an invisible trapeze.

Your eye catches mine
in a practiced,

subtle wink.

Unsympathetic
        to your body's
protest—your muscles

swimming in lactate,
        your bone
        fusing to sinew—

the instructor's
                lilting voice
rolls you through agony:

*Can you twist
more . . . like this? More
toward the sky. Yes
the arm. We must see
the arm. Everything
must flow to sky.*

Hold . . .

        hold . . .

hold.

This is how
        you describe it:

your mind, trained
      suffers tremors so
your body won't have to.

Charcoal and pastels
      crumble along your skin,
vicariously fondle
      your hips and thighs.

Your lips
          succumb
to a dozen fingers'
            touch. Studied
hands map your ribs,

sweep your small taut
            breasts up toward
the slender neck. Later
                  you confess

I have had lovers
      who knew less
of me—and
            I have lost
them that way.

Halo in Decline

Paul Delaroche's La Jeune Martyre

In death, there appears
    as if by providence
a golden oval, circling
       over
           your head
as you float
in the rolling Tiber.

Not God, but Paul
has christened
    a halo to cast
a glacial shine
    to your cheek.

The world around you
is thick cast high
    by camel hair
and steady, steady hand.

Minutes after
    Diocletian's tyranny
married your corpse
to current still warm
enough to steam
    rivulets across
the river's roiling skin

Paul summons
      expensive oils,
      overpriced brushes
to petrify you to canvas.

Each man, resolute,
believes the other's
heavy-handed strokes
          damn you.

A hundred years later
your body is still
drifting past moored boats.

There is ritual
evident in your wrists
cross-bound, roped

to your waist;
    every line of you
slopes down
    into the darkness,
shimmering.

Driven sweet,
the day bitters, glows
and trickles along
    your tongue beckoning throat.

Your hair, once autumn's
      great mane,
is now dulled and wintered.

The frigid bedding
          brilliantly peaks
your rosy hue,
          your insolence.

Dare I: your flint and spark
snuffed by the emperor's
night, but no less so
by Delaroche's ambition.

Despite both men, you
      radiate still
          that damnable
resolve, irreverent

martyr's smile
      that surely hastened
the hammer's fall.

Mississippi Barbecue

*"Postcard #80" from Without Sanctuary
exhibit*

Sliced away and soaking
   in jars, the sweet parts:
      tongue
      eyes
      genitals saved
for luck and souvenirs.

The Negro ablaze, back
arched as if in ecstasy.

Having lingered
   once too long
on a white woman's face

he is reclined,
   bullet-ridden, languid
on the blistering pyre.

Centered in the tableau
still life posed for
the cameraman's steady eye.

Twice, the magnesium
flash sparks
through the dapper crowd:

27

two score fedora & bonnet
crowned heads
    lean into sight line.
Swamp-rot
    and bloodlust crawl
through the eyes.

Later, there's potato
salad & sweet cold tea.

Soaked in blood, soaked
    in piss, the hunting sack
crumpled into itself
at fire's edge, smolders.

Rumor is the postcards
will be a dollar.

The body
now chalking toward pristine
is left to the children

lipless, its grin
crackling in tinder.

The sheriff's
        youngest boy
    rattles a cane 'round
the ribcage 'til it caves
    like a miner's tomb.

A fiery halo
blossoms on the chin.
Bits of charred
     flesh flake away
     float lazily
on the night breeze.

Flame-struck and
       spellbound,
the pastor
   sucks absently

a rib bone, prays
    the children understand
the need
     for cleansing.

—for Kwame Dawes

Settling the Score

In a libretto
    there is a song
        for every kill.

I hum Puccini
until my heart snaps.

At my desk, fingers
curled around the hilt

of my pencil—
I recite the edicts
    of my creed:

      This is opera.
      I, a composer.
      The character is female:
      She must die.

I have no stomach
    to rescind the life
gifted her by the librettist.

Today she will
      be my Cio-Cio-San,
calling me to extinguish
the red lantern
    above her head.

I hum myself
            into the scene
to finish her off

take stage as *Kabuki*
                onnagata: man
of silk, pearls,
            and scented waters.

Scarlet obi constricts
      my gut; skin
blanched; lips
                bitten ripe
as dove hearts;
        thick smile cocked
behind a bone-
        colored fan.

Outlined in vibrant
silk she drifts
      the stage, trailing

a litany of spotlights
            and parenthetical
phrases. I follow

      feverishly recast
my brain, now as
      a poisoned adder
coiled like an angry rope
inside my skull.

The finale arrives. I
have scored
      the full libretto
   onto the tip
         of my lead-
graphite sword.

When she turns to solo
I stagger her down
   an octave, render

her flightless, painless
      no more, always
the woman dies.

              —for Regie Gibson

MIDDAY

Six poems based on the painting
*Aspects of Negro Life #62: Song of
the Towers,* by Aaron Douglas

A man travels the world over in search of
what he needs and returns home to find it.

—GEORGE MOORE

Growing Wings

Listen:
they had to name Jazz
before they could pull
    Armstrong's tongue
through his horn

stamp it to vinyl.
I itch for my turn.

It's guttural, instinct
    hatched from marrow,
insisting I turn prodigal:

be Be-Bop
    bound catch
the Trane clattering
    up my spine.

Father sent tractors
    and oak-root
to hammer
       my feet to soil.

I sent Sonny
        &
      Holiday to kiss
    at the gates,
gum the hinges.

37

Cursing birthright
    and family, I dialed
up *Song of the Towers*

Harlem's taboo
      of euphony
and Steel
and God-
        Crazed sweetness.

In a month I'm cutting
    heads with razor
blades and mirrors staking
my muses. Cravings
      outmuscled dreams.

I hock my axe
for work gloves
    and hard hat. Winter

careens me into hunger
      and shakes; my
body hollowed out,

filled with a crazed hum.
    Everything
I know is hunger
      or regret.

Marking Time Blues

Monday morning
    my car quivers
outside
    the mechanic's
open bay knowing

once in, it may
         never roll
out again. It shudders

thick
oils darkening
     pavement.

I cycle uphill
    to work
hunched over
      handlebars
like over a prison meal.

Just past the deli,
    the chain
rusted, convulses
    like a snake
    pinched beneath
a shovel's blade

with its last breath
  growing angry
biting into my calf.

  Blood swells
like a river,
  the shallow
chasm in my leg.

Working late
  I'm jonesing,
bandaged, sweating

drifting off
  beneath dim
warehouse lighting.

Once,
  dream-walking

Coleman
  Hawkins stepped
out of a crevice
in the wall,
  eyes bloodshot.

He wanted to know
  how we got here.

Not going home is already like death.

—E. CATHERINE TOBLER,
"VANISHING ACT"

The Homecoming: Prodigal

I dream of sweetgrass and grunting tractors,
how the South can linger, unscratchable.

Momma still dreams an oak anchors my spine.
She can't see there's rot hollowing the flesh.

Memories clutched too tight twist to kudzu
and crabgrass. Creek water stills, turns stagnant.

Miles of barbed wire rust against my skin;
jittery eyes squint against the sun's glare.

It's Momma's fault I've come home. Not seeing
the horror I've become, she lets me in.

The Homecoming: Brother

Li'l bro, you come home scratching track scars,
jagged symbols; even a blind man can

trace your history. I hear the Lime House
refuses more of the ghosts you carry.

So you store them, bundled up with box twine,
a dry tinder to spark the grief you spread.

Looks like you still slave to the hate of us.
This farm, scorched and cratered, remembers you;

I prophesized your return from shadows
on the fields; curses darkening the sky.

The Homecoming: Father

My son, I wish your back unbroken from
the weight in your eyes, body a question

mark of sorrow, hostage to past laments.
I wish black sheep could be free of mythos.

I wish your fingers clean of tangled knots,
the one heirloom you didn't steal from me.

I forgive the moon for lighting your path,
the Good Lord for not troubling your compass,

the train's whistle for trumpeting you back,
even the street signs for pointing you home.

Never Come Home Again

I sit in the back
     row of church
singing along with tremors
   that score my life
and body.

The pew strains
     beneath my hands
twitching through

a hallelujah chorus.

I drink communion
     sweat blood,
gasping hunched
   over my lap, knowing

       there's a kill
switch jutting
     from my coat
pocket: silver flask
dulled by leathery
fingers.
     Touch.

Preacher raises
   his hand, a hymn
carries the room

like crow flight
      over a bush.

I pick up my hat
    set it low, scuttle
out the back
down the steps.

The corner bus stop
    is a toad squatting
in sunlight.

By noon
    I'm sleeping
off my tremors
    on the North-
bound
    Nine,
back to Harlem,

dreaming

I'm a blind wisteria
    stalk, climbing
an ivory tower.

MIDAFTERNOON

Brought to these knees, in this light,
this heat, how the sun blanches my back;
or is it a flaying, and I, thoughts pouring
into sand, welcome this stinging,
the copper-stench flood of revelation?

After

The swiftly arcing sun now splits
our naked backs with light, ruined
our touch, now frantic: blindfish
slipping through a canyon fissure.

Your tresses, tendriled & tousled,
sift light from dust risen against
the pale, pale walls. Shadows slip down
your nape, seeking sanctuary.

Nothing crazed can snarl, then rattle
midday into morning's crevice—
the clock spills through our trembling touch.
I sift anxiously through ashes,

façade dwindling, unprepared for
your whisper—a thin, graying wisp—
No, it's done, your tongue weighted down
with crows, wings heavy with fresh snow.

The Argument

What I remember
is your head—
an old Victorian,
stained-
    glass eyelids
high, unshuttered.

When the storm
broke your pulley
ropes snapped,

windows slammed
down paint
            flakes
crumbled,
papering your cheeks;

Tell me you
    remember
everything not said.

You say
there was sky
  emptying through
my tongue's fist:

Circling us both,
    what we meant
    lumbers
alongside
what we said, not
    recognizing
       each other;

one nurses a limp
       neither
of us
will acknowledge.

Malaise

Your feet moored
    to autumn
planking
    empty boardwalk.

I snap pictures
        rocks
wish-washed clean
in tidal pools.

Summer has moored
itself over the great
    unwashed horizon.

I snap pictures
      seagulls
anchored
    to stone clouds.

You want a remembrance
of the two gulls
        skidding
over the placid surf.
I fake snapping
a picture. Upset
    about something
earlier, forgotten.

I am reminded
        how
everything is not
a poem
        today or ever:

not the dead fiddler
crab (Trojan horse
    shell of maggots)
            gracing
the shoreline.

I have a camera today
    proving this nothing
is everything
        worth writing about:

the turtle, back-wobbled
by the Doberman
slobbering,
        claw-prodded.
Interesting, yes,

but not a metaphor
            for anything
save that even

        death can lose
its way, sunning
on a lackluster beach
        unnoticed
if the haze is just so.

Taking Stock

At 44, I'm shocked
        by my cubist
reflection, as if
in a funhouse mirror:

a grandfather twice,
memories crisscrossing
    my body, scars
like soldiers
    who died where
they fell.

Yet I'm still playing
my game, wondering

what it would mean
to have been someone's
son, cherished
    in a father's eyes.

Scalp thinning
    I contemplate my
tender skull—perfect
        container
for this unresolved
mind-thing

calculating
the ever-increasing
    spots on my skin

canvas, light-damaged
    and weathered
a little more each year.

Unsympathetic, the mirror
    notes whimsical
squiggles escaping

    my eyes, bastard
worms fleeing
    a sinking ship.

My ten crooked fingers:
clutching, releasing
    one straight
enough to be despised
        by the others.
(I give it
    sanctuary daily
behind mundane
    objects: pencils
        can openers
    paper cups.) Taste

    buds worn to nubs, lips
cracked stones. Fat
    pouches cling
to my waist, time
        bombs

jiggling
        in every supple
fold.   God!
this demitasse
of bone and gristle.

While I searched elder
      faces for light,
         what precious
juices time
      has boiled away.

One Summer

I could only hold
my children in poems.
I thought
        us cursed, a witch
tormenting our name.

Scoliosis
        rioted
along my youngest
daughter's spine. I slept
for a week beneath

gray walls and ceilings,
        seven sunsets
                spiraling
over the horizon. While

in another room
my oldest daughter, son
        sliced from her,
shuffled gingerly

as if over coals
        and broken glass
from bed to bathroom

holding her belly
        both our hearts
in such small hands.

Shrunken into a corner,
      my son—he
and his guitar strapped
to a long-sung tonality

trying to ratchet
down a single note
        for loneliness.

In my worst dreams
we are Icarus, winging
across a rusted desert.

Next scene, they
        are gut-shot—
one, two, three
black wings flailing

    against broken air,
composite
      scream vibrating
through my bones.

I turn, not looking
      and leap, hoping
to be Father-God-Savior

but I carry two
           cursed hands
that can't possibly hold
    the explosions
blossoming in my chest.

In my best dreams
our fingernails
         actually touch
before we all fall.

Perspective, Wanting

I don't know why grace
adorns every killing field:

the hanged slave's pirouette
against the oak's indifference;

the perfect, trebling E climbing
the smokestack in Auschwitz;

the mantis's orchestration
of blissful decapitation;

the dust spirals in moonlight as
the door hushes closed behind you.

What I Meant

My tongue has walked
you down that warm
      privileged path

To the riotous pool
      where aching peonies
            giant-headed sunflowers
            and plum-dark
tumbling poinsettias
      luxuriate in vigil,
I am not with you.

Still, my mind shocked
      into terrifying bliss
stupefied, dazzled
has not completely abandoned
            the here-now.

No.

(swallowing) Engaged
      in bacchanal ritual
I am all
      my senses, saturnalia,
      NOT elsewhere, but
in you: To put it

(Curtly) in your heart,
      Dear Woman.

or

(Coarsely) Miles
had trumpet,
      I have . . .

Here, let's try

(Bluntly) ricocheting
     from tongue to clitoris
is a new alphabet.

Listen:
     this is your name.

DUSK

. . . as all the usual sunset colors
break over his face,
he starts up singing again,
same as every night, same song: loneliness
by starlight . . .

—CARL PHILLIPS, "RIDING WESTWARD"

The (Un)doing

First, the Mississippi
     went dark   pitch&acid,
so we rolled
     back its name.

~~Miss~~   ~~I~~   ~~ssi~~   ~~ppi~~

The sky hung
               scorched
cloudless: last

     blade of grass
stunted
          as the sun; last
tree charcoaled
                    twisted.

We now knew
the truth of extinction:
seeing
          we mistook
for knowing. Having
named the world,
we thought it immortal.

We unwalked the ~~roads~~,
fled underground
bringing
    everything not dead.

Hunched in caves
        we set about
untaking it all.

Our skin turned
        sickly glow.
We erased the shine
with sackcloth
        then undid
the name: ~~sack~~

We unwrote dictionaries.
    Unspined encyclopedias,
words ashing in bonfires.

Unspun a gyroscope
into a chunk
      of metal craving
attention.

~~Yesterday~~, we unlearned
       our own ~~names~~,
breaking pacts
    with language
until all was new again.

Next, went to work
      on flesh. Plucked
~~hair~~, peeled
back ~~tongues~~

unhinged limbs until
      we were torsos
dark in bloom
    dumbstruck
saving our last breath
      to unlight candles.

Devoid of ~~hands~~,
    we gutted the last
~~clocks~~
~~with our teeth~~.

Holding Patterns

A single snow
goose flying south
against
    a storm
of unmigrating wings.

There is fruit smashed
into his feathers

lemon peelings stuck
in his nostrils.

His compass dizzy
with orange, tiny
        brain floating
in a sea of citrus.

There is a loneliness
        to his call.

At pond's edge the boy:
mind crippled
   by the endless
        indignations

his pinch-faced, bifocaled
days bring him.

His compass, too,
          is dead
needle drowning
in loneliness
and abandonment.

Goose smashes into boy.
Both bodies unclench
for the first time

in weeks. Over
the small ridge
          of cattails and reeds
comes the boy's father.

His son's cry drums
          his ears. He runs,
a hammer creasing
          cattails. The reeds

do not claim him,
          his thudding boots
          his overalls
          his thick neck
sweat trickling slowly.

They fall away—
spring
back behind him.

His hand opens.
A phone thuds
          to the moist ground.

From the tinny speaker,
the voice of his elder
    half-blind neighbor:

Your barn is burning
Oh God what happened
    to your sprinklers
The flames are jumping
to the roof of the house!

House or son.
Barn or son.

For the first time
since his wife
    abandoned them
he chooses son.

The angry phone
    yelping
      from the mud.

The father sees
silhouetted, the goose
wings beating
    his son's face.

The boy's flailing
arms, tortured
    wail escaping lips.

The phone screeches
across the bow
    of the breeze:

Your house!
Your house!
Oh God
    your house!

    Running.

The father knows
    how the fire
must have begun:

There is a lantern
burning   always
in the high window
of his barn where

he sleeps nightly
    in the loft
    in the hay
shivering
with the breeze
from the pond

    a flannel shirt
perfumed and balled
    beneath his head.

It will be lit
forever until she returns.

The lantern left
    alone, at the mercy
of the breeze.

The lantern left alone,
at the mercy of the goose
nightly drawn
      to the light
and the soft scent of grain

the one true warmth
in the cold spring nights.

It must have been
the goose he shooed
away each night
protecting his oily-
bright promise

to his vanished wife.

The goose and its
goose-wing clipping
the lantern over
    into hay
    onto the scented shirt.

Yes, it must have been.
    The flames had
no choice but
      burn the promise
      burn the barn
      burn the house.

Now fast-forward:
past the father red-
    faced on his knees
strangling the goose.

Fast-forward past
the dying goose,
his compass still
              awash
in orange and lime

neck bent
        a wicked angle.

Fast-forward past the son
    curled into the reeds
that do not claim
him, his tortured cries.

Fast-forward all
    the way to the trembling

father scarred with
scarred son silent, both
in the truck.

Never does it occur
to the boy
        the goose
was the same he crept
up on days before
and smashed
        maliciously
with overripe fruit.

Never
does the father think
the strangled goose
    is the same one
he chased away   nightly
from his lantern,
      his promise.

And they shouldn't.

The goose
that attacked the
    boy is not
the same one
      he attacked,
was not the same
as the father's
nightly visitor.

Rounding the last corner
to their neighborhood
        they see
not their own
    but the barn
of an adjacent house afire.

Still, pulling
into their driveway
the father sees
    his loft window
with no light. Lantern

extinguished. Not

a goose, but
        a gusting breeze
        has taken
    his promise.

His head sinks
to the steering wheel.

Half a state away,
    an old farm truck
wings down

the highway beneath
the moon.

The windows are down.
The driver is humming.
Her hair is awash
    in wind and night.

—*for Charles Harper Webb*

Grasshopper Blues

By the time winter
bites chunks
    from autumn's ass,
I'm done bargaining
with shingles, begging
my roof for one more season.

I've got a pry bar, a ladder,
and a twitch the roof
can't help but notice—
there's *malice*
    in this turn of events.

Curses fixed, grinning, I'm
    halfway between rungs
when
a jagged shingle wings
toward my head spinning
    like a maple seed copter.

And quick-as-you-please, dead
autumn now
    sounds like clatter-
clatter-crowbar-clunk
    me chest down in heavy-
handed manzanita, hiding
the foundation's base-rot.

My face, deep
in topsoil
    drainage-hell marsh,

finds a rock.

Dark, sick roses bloom
across my vision, succulent

in their flowing grace;
meandering scarlet rivulets
twist through grass.

In the chestnut branches
    by the overgrown
koi pond, crows guffaw

ants SAVE!

      Ben Franklin SAVES!

Jesus EVEN!

I can't help notice as
the blood
    parades down
my forehead, shirt,
      pants, et cetera

coagulating between my toes
    my right foot, shoe
            lost,

isn't it just wonderful
the way snow
       doesn't give
a fuck when
    suddenly falling
it raises the stakes
before the first hand is dealt.

                  —for Mella

Thief

You are everywhere
    in my house;
everything I touch.

Your scent
wound
    through clothes
you sit and coil
          uncoil

    Strike, sink
      into my wrist
and slip
    beneath my skin.

For hours
    your shadow climbs
        the back fence.

A cat curls
    into a calico
stone beside the planter.

Morning creaks
through the back gate.
Dogs sniff the air,
whimper as you steal

away
leaping rooftop
    to tree branch
        to horizon.

I was not
    dreaming.
There was a burglar.

She stole
    everything I tried
to give

    fondled everything
    too big to take.
        Her eyes were brown
or green   *hazel*
            perhaps
      mirrored.

She towered above
    me. Her fingernails
    caressed my nipples.

Her lips drowned me
her tongue
    a rain forest.

Messages from the Ether

Your first text put
    you in *The Decameron*
tracking Boccaccio

through love's sickness
    deep moist erotica.

You leave no name,
            your number
unrecognizable.

Weeks later I'm in
    City Lights coaxing
Jane Shore to raise

the trapeze artist
    once more
from concrete and straw.

I read
    you are hours away
from winging above

my head through fog
        and spring
on your way

to Hong Kong. That night
    I dream dragon-
smoke scripting
       my name
against a flame-red sky.

A month later
    Man on Wire
    traps you
between two towers

glued to a wire
       swaying over
a man-made chasm.

I'm in bed nursing
a knee swollen around
an ACL stretched
       to disbelief.

You say Petit left you
    dizzy, mind
spiraling unhinged

      above the rubble
      that will be
         decades later

dragging glass and ruin
    beneath autumn's
indifference.

Three months pass
    before I ask who
you are   careful

of the fragility
      of names
      and faces
made concrete
      easily shattered.

It's Eva you reply
    From Boston
    From the Fogg
    From theater
and poetry reaching

through static
      and distance.

Eva, my friend
      as I write this poem

Boston should be
past the flowering
           season
      heat hovering

      over the Charles
dragonflies rustling.

I imagine you
sitting
      lotus-style
on the north bank

hair tied
     a knot that trails
   down your back.

   You lean over
your phone concentrating
   on every letter

     and symbol before
  winging them
      across ether.

         —for Eva Ng

Glass

I vowed
      never again
to cross that street.

But the snake charmer
      laid his flute
along my spine.

Sodium light
      painted
my shadow crooked
      across the restaurant's
            plate glass

my breath quickening
against the pane.

Inside,
      mint teas
      incense
      dark spices
tinted air.

A belly dancer
timed finger cymbals
and a coined sash

to a *bağlama's**
    dulcet strumming.

    Handwoven
tapestries
    thickened the walls

tugging
at connecting studs.

Couches crouched
    low and sensuous

every divan and ottoman
                 adorned
with scented pillows
and entwined legs.

She and I were
    only here once

I reminded myself.

Still, the music pulsed
the glass
      beneath my fingers

as hookah pipes
      rose and fell

like empires,
    like longing.

              —for Yusef

*The *bağlama* is a fundamental instrument in Turkish folk music.

Rebirth

Waiting until dusk
the Blackhole climbed down
    from the heavens and through
the stonecutter's window.

On its vast back it toted
a knapsack full
    of the everything
it had yet to digest:

        a porcelain doll's blank stare
        twin pulsars from a distant galaxy
        an omelet-encrusted spatula
        parapets from a high castle wall.

Having squeezed into the shape
of the once-tall stonecutter
                the Blackhole sat
at the kitchen table
in precisely the cutter's way:
    hunched over
    knees together
    staring across

to where his wife would sit
if she was yet
home from tending
        the master's garden.

On the table lay
a marble spinning top carved
from a block smuggled
	from the master's keep.

It was the top
and the promise of spinning
that drew the Blackhole
from its perch in heaven.

The stonecutter spent
two years
cutting marble slabs
for his master's ballroom.

Shoulders circled slowly,
		polishing stone
until his hands were gnarled knots
he no longer recognized—
	lumps of sinew
and bone hanging
			from his arms.

The master's daughter
	would turn 18 soon;
a woman's age.

Her desire was to spin
on marble slick
	as wet glass, spin
like sunset rolling
	down the royal garden tree line.

It was, too, the promise
of this spinning that drew
the Blackhole from its cubbyhole
in the ceiling of the universe,
climbing
      down
galaxy
      after
galaxy

to the stonecutter's kitchen.

All winter long
the stonecutter cut
   marble and polished.
Set slabs in place
and polished. Grouted
cracks and polished.

Occasionally he coveted
      small, dull chunks
to his kitchen
where, by candlelight,
he set his hands
      to releasing dolls
and houses
   horses and chariots
from their marble
prisons. And,
      just once,
a perfectly shaped top.

The top, in its almost
        realized potential
to spin, reminded

the Blackhole of a galaxy
it devoured five million
        years before.

It was the shining
marble top, the ceremony
        of carving,
                the memory of the galaxy,
the soon-to-spin daughter
                that drew
the Blackhole
to the stonecutter's kitchen.

It was, too, the spinning
                the anniversary
        of womanhood
and shine—
        the small chunk
of stone the cutter
        stole away in his wagon.

The marble
now whittled down
        to a sleek
shining top
                toppled
on its side, wobbled

on the cutter's breadboard
as the Blackhole shook
      the table
with its many solar
            systems shaped
into hands.

For the sake of ceremony
for spinning
            for the austere
birthplaces of marble

the Blackhole opened
its mouth and released
            the devoured galaxy.
Let it spin down
                  and light
upon the top
      righting it
            setting it spinning again
on the stonecutter's breadboard.

A planet in the galaxy
      awoke, continued on
as if nothing
            had happened

the people making bread
            making love
      spinning
            cutting marble.

They now live
　　　on the marble top
helping it spin
　　　　　to cut a new language
into the wooden
　　　　breadboard.

In their tongue,
the word *spin* also means
"once we dreamed . . ."

　　　　　　　　　　—for Toni Wynn